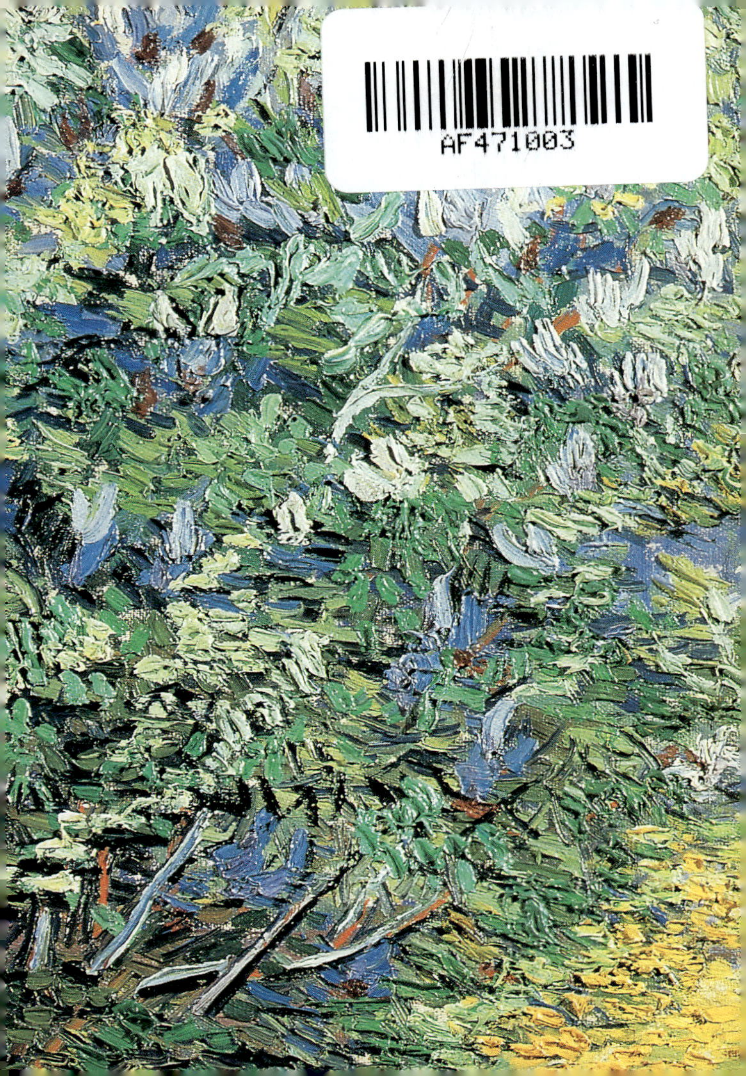
AF471003

Other giftbooks by Exley:
Klimt Notebook   Renoir Book of Days
Monet Notebook   Sunflowers A Birthday Book
Cézanne Notebook

Published simultaneously in 1996 by Exley Publications in Great Britain, and Exley Giftbooks in the USA.
Copyright © Helen Exley 1996

12 11 10 9 8 7 6 5 4 3 2 1
ISBN 1-85015-780-4

All rights reserved. No part of this publication may be reproduced or transmitted in any form or by any means, electronic or mechanical, including photocopy, recording or any information storage and retrieval system without permission in writing from the Publisher.
Pictures selected by Helen Exley.
Designed by Pinpoint Design.
Picture research by Image Select, London.
Typeset by Delta, Watford.
Printed in Hungary.
Exley Publications would like to thank the following organizations for permission to reproduce the pictures and the border details in this book: Archiv für Kunst, Edimedia, Giraudon, Scala, The Bridgeman Art Library.
Cover: *Thatched Cottages at Cordeville*, Auvers-sur-Oise, Musée d'Orsay, Paris; endpapers: *Lilla*, Hermitage Museum, St. Petersburg; title page: *Thatched Cottages at Cordeville*, Auvers-sur-Oise, Musée d'Orsay, Paris

Exley Publications Ltd, 16 Chalk Hill, Watford, Herts, WD1 4BN, UK.
Exley Giftbooks, 232 Madison Avenue, Suite 1206, NY 10016, USA.

Vincent Van Gogh (1853-1890)

Van Gogh lived as an art dealer, a lay preacher and a tramp before deciding to become an artist. He used vivid tones and swirling brushstrokes to heighten reality, and to express "the terrible inner passions." His personal life was marred by these passions: he suffered bouts of depression and hallucinations. In 1888, after a quarrel with the artist Gauguin, he cut off his own ear. After this he entered an asylum for the insane, where he continued to paint at a prolific pace. However, subsequent breakdowns culminated in his suicide at the scene of his last painting, the ominous "Crows over Wheatfield".

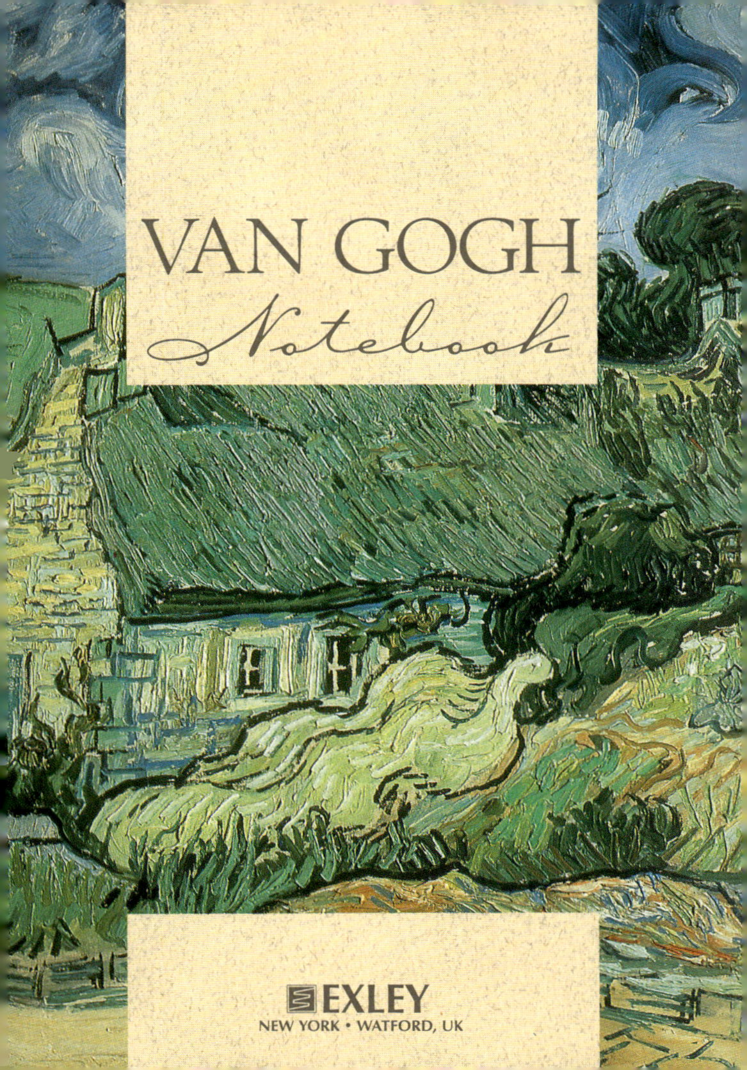
VAN GOGH
Notebook
EXLEY
NEW YORK • WATFORD, UK

Starry Night on the Rhine, 1888
Private Collection

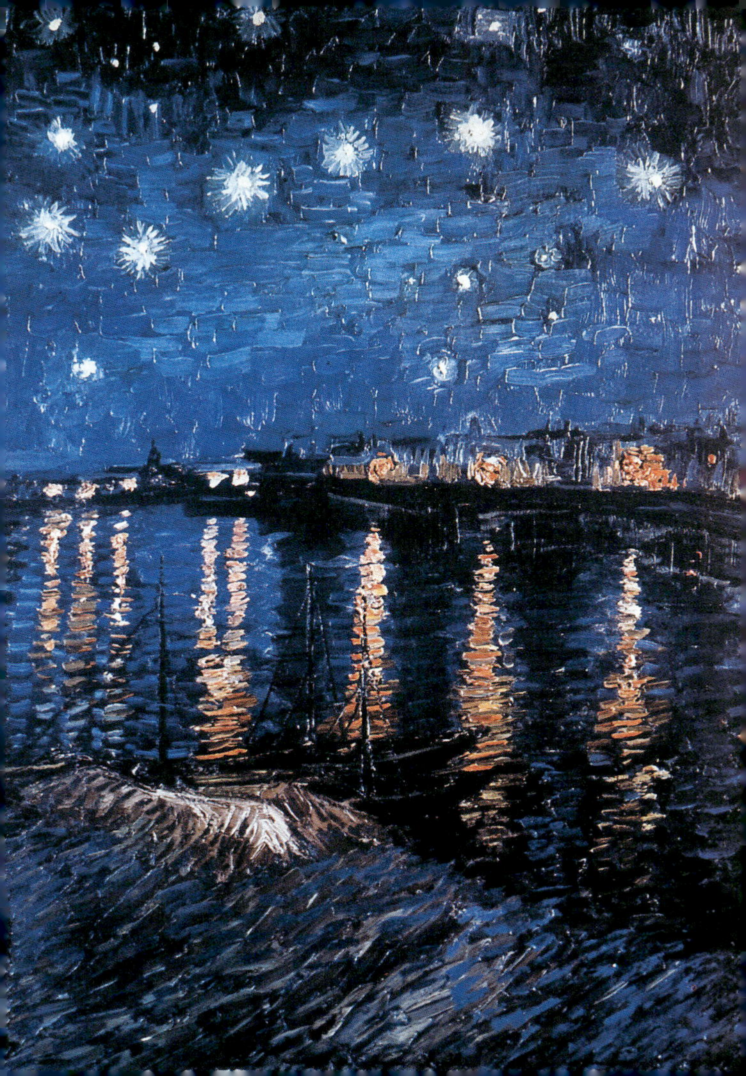

Kazbaz.

While the world is sleeping

I know you're out there, as I watch your candle burning low

I remember your smiles, and also, your special quiet moments.

But I cannot feel a happiness.

• Maybe I should, and whilst I am trying,

My feelings are more that of crying.

Sometimes I need you, maybe just for a moment,

But that is the moment I know you're not there.

• I hope one day I can smile, and know,

That when your candle gives off that glow,

Flickering brightly, like you used to be

Special to all, not just me.

February 1997.

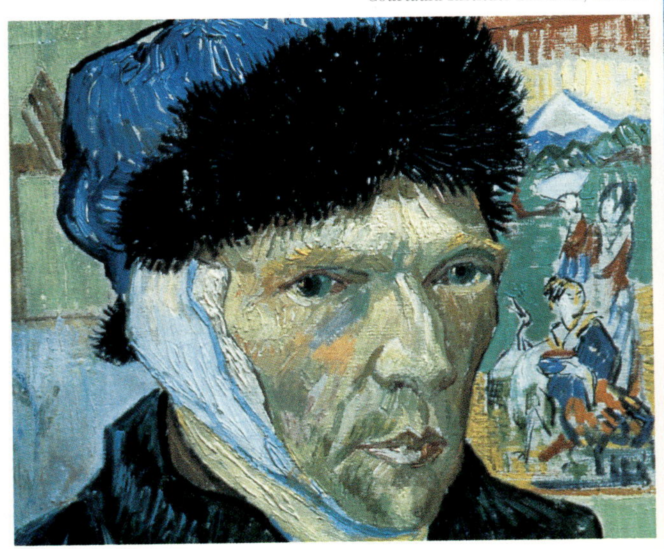

Self-Portrait with Bandaged Ear, 1889
Courtauld Institute Galleries, London

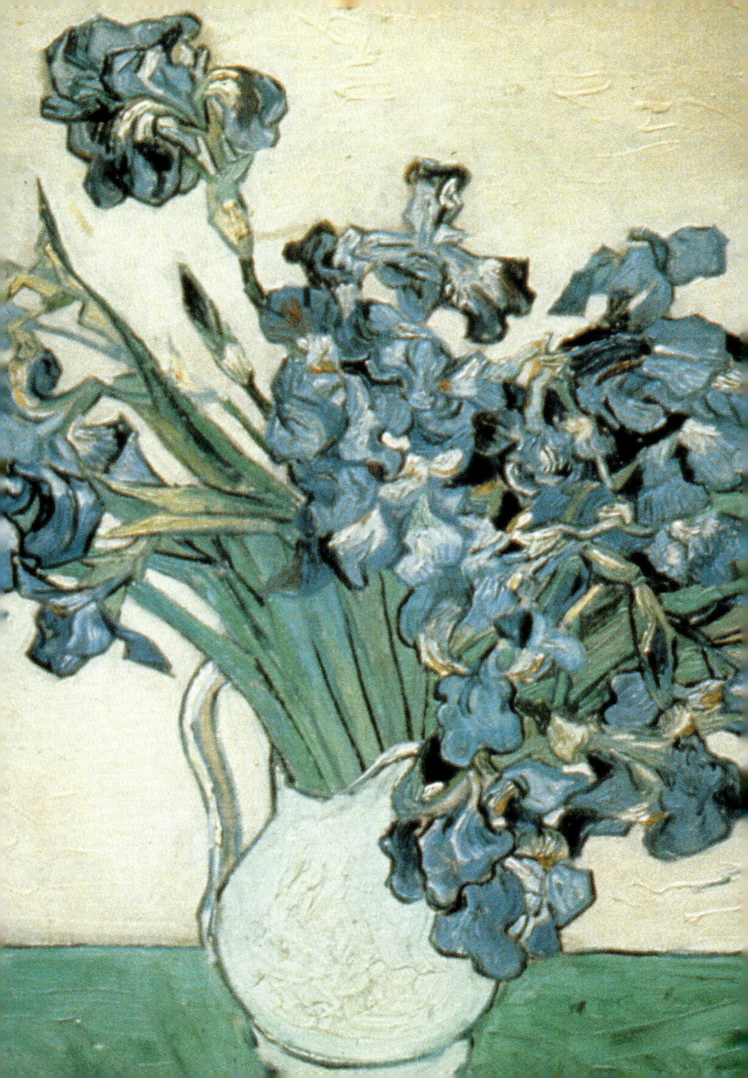

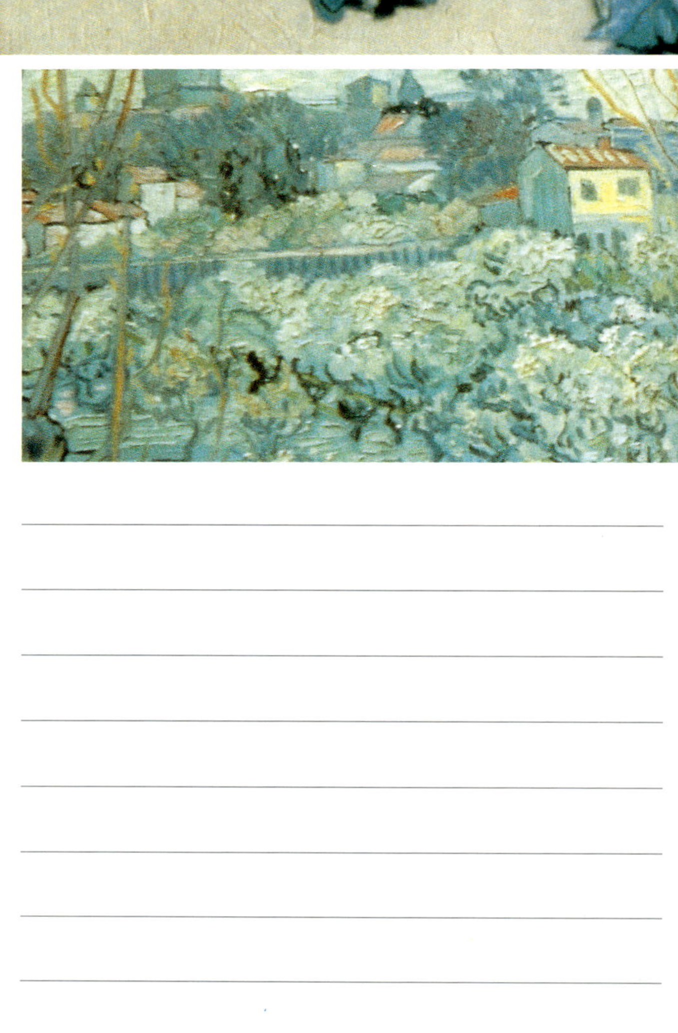

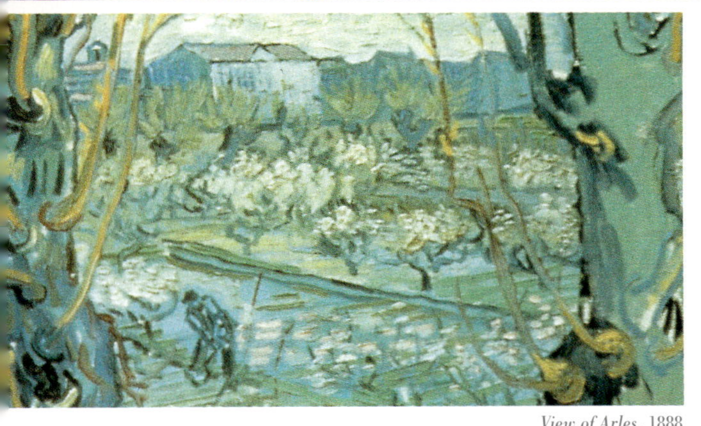

View of Arles, 1888
Munich

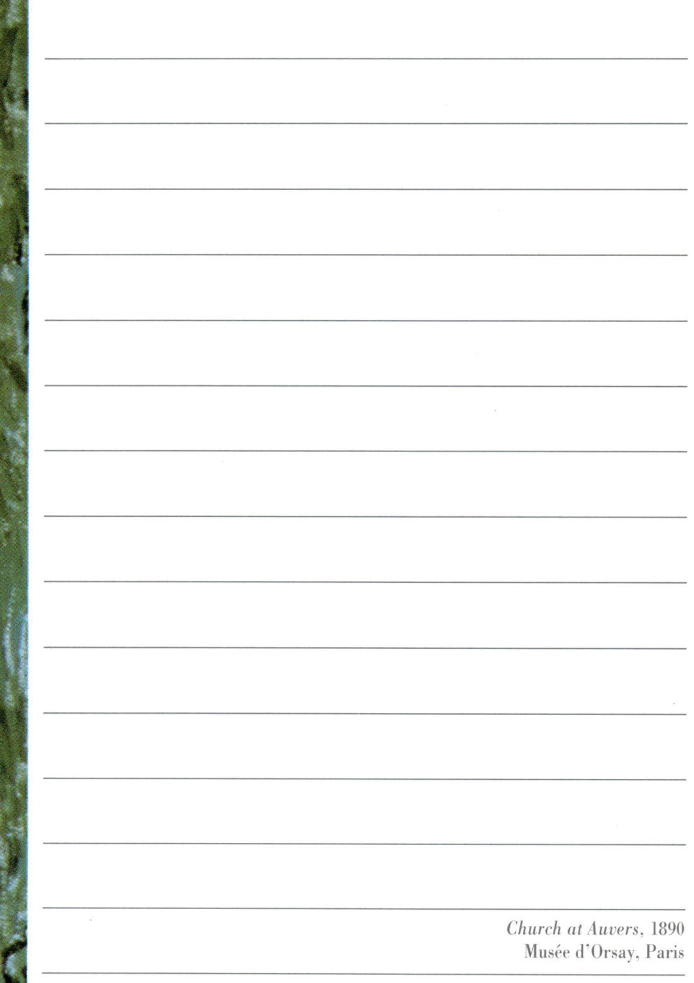

Church at Auvers, 1890
Musée d'Orsay, Paris

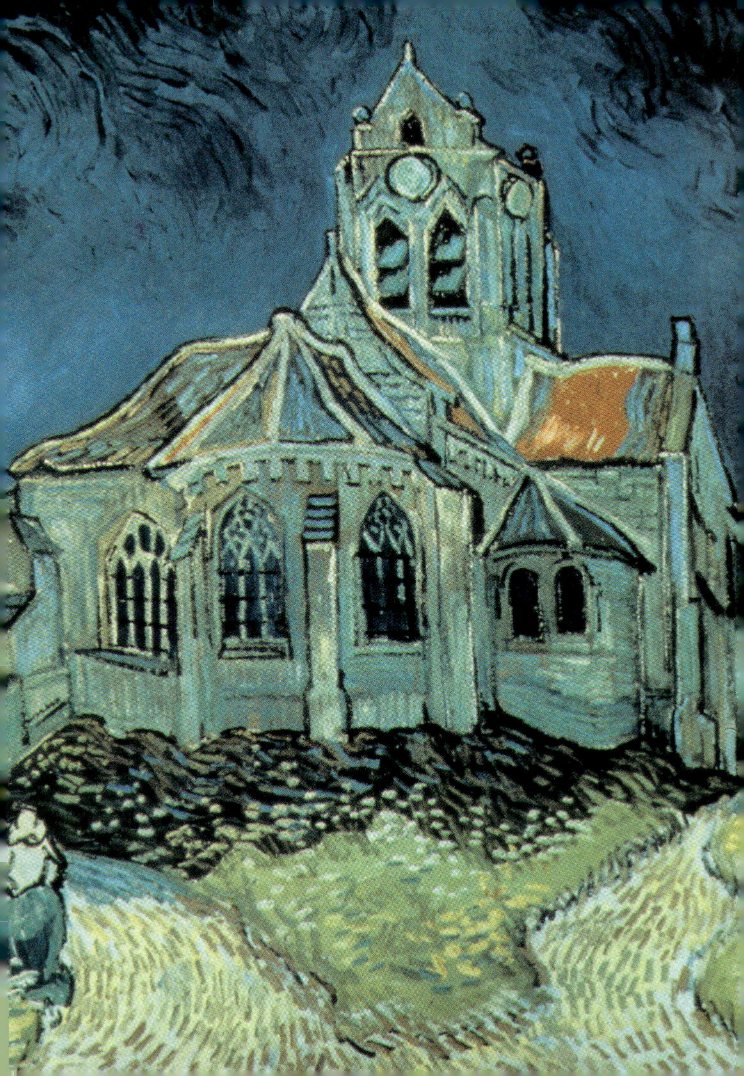

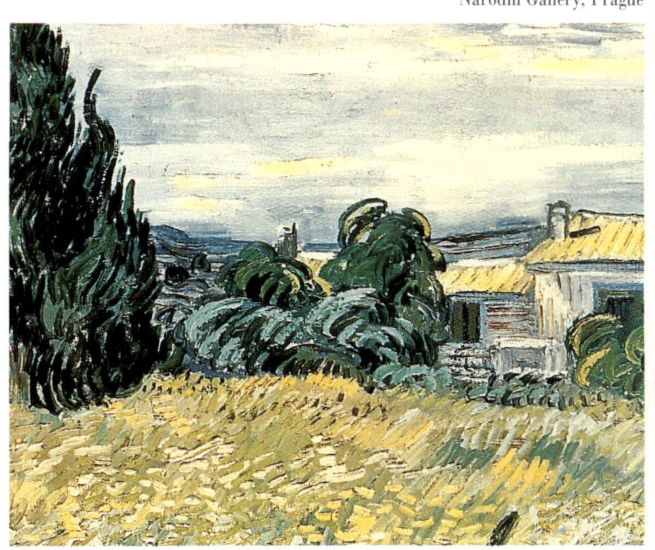

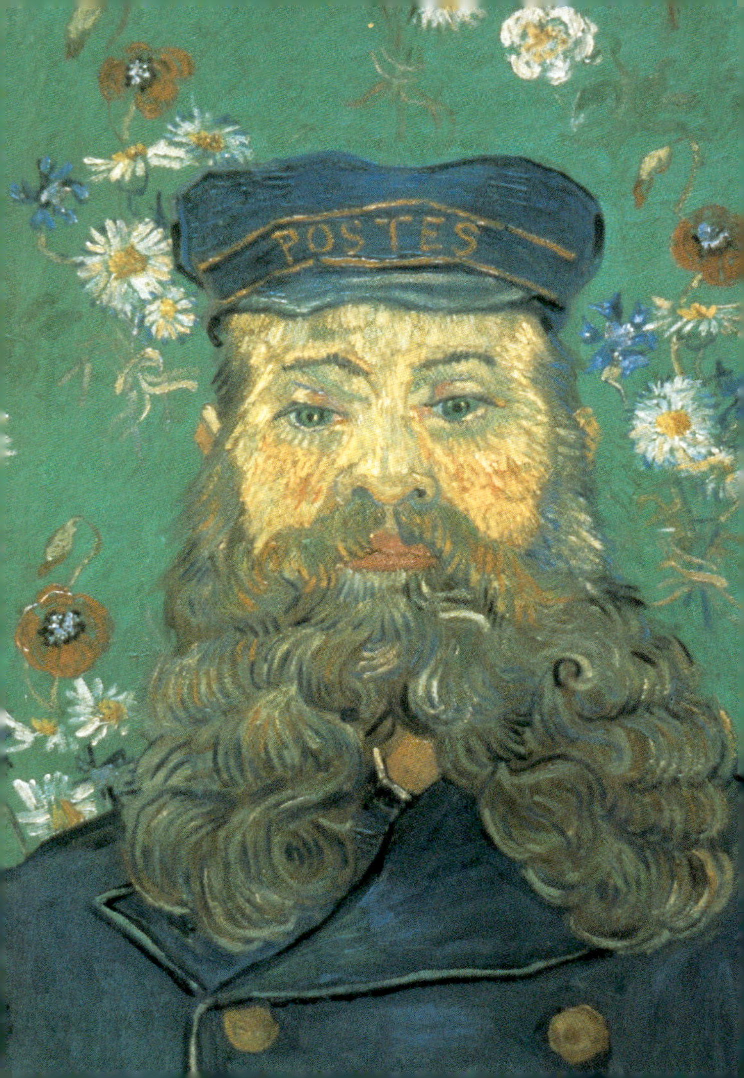
POSTES

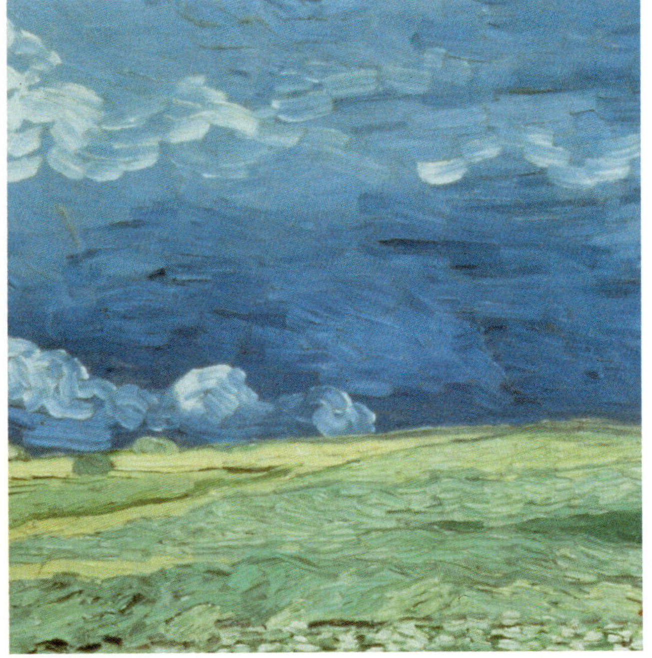

Field Under Thunderclouds, 1890
Rijksmuseum Vincent Van Gogh, Amsterdam

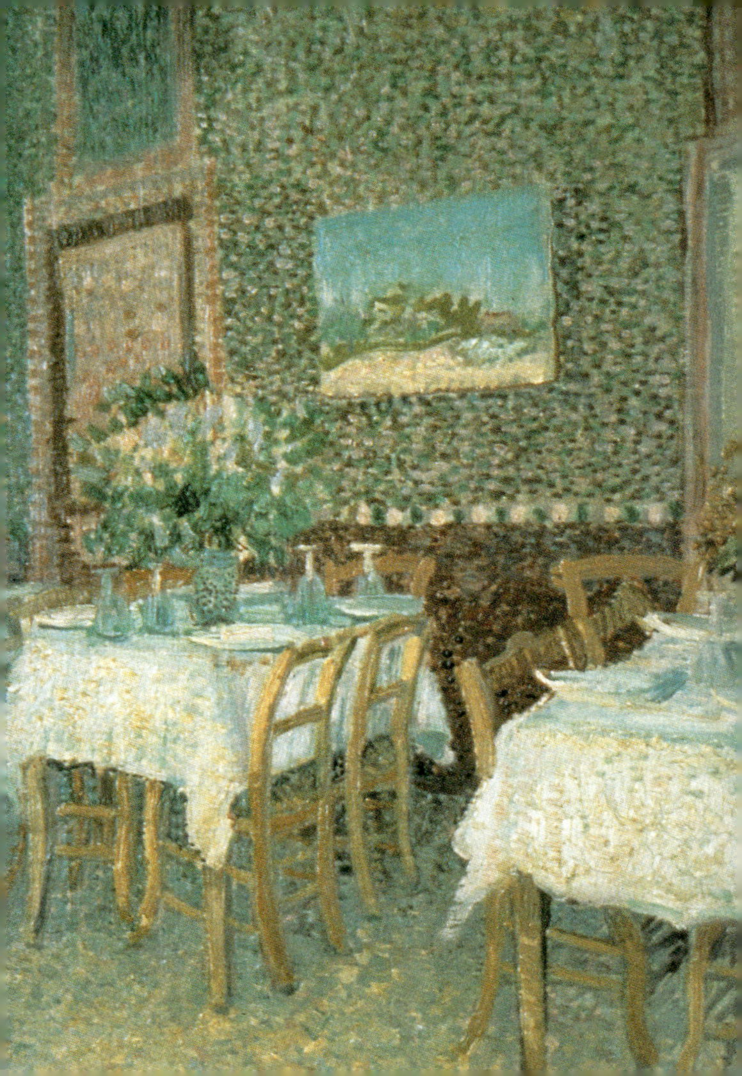

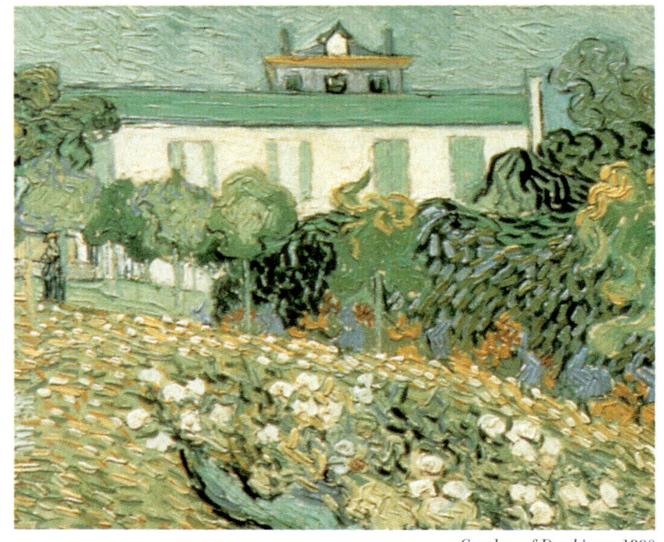

Garden of Daubigny, 1890
Private Collection

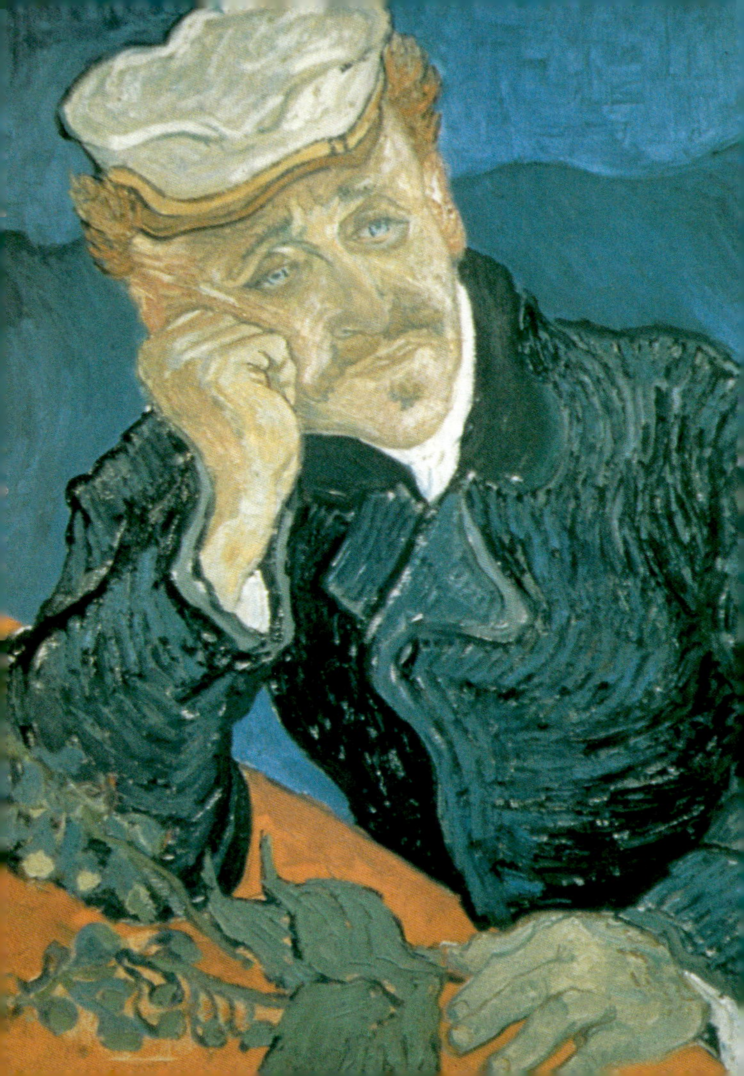

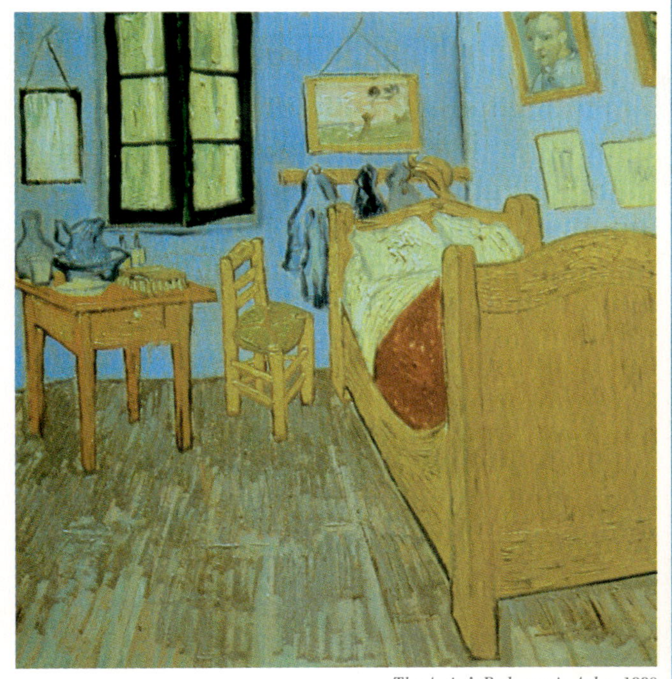

The Artist's Bedroom in Arles, 1889
Musée d'Orsay, Paris

Cafe Terrace at Night, Place du Forum in Arles, 1888
Rijksmuseum Kroeller-Muller, Otterlo

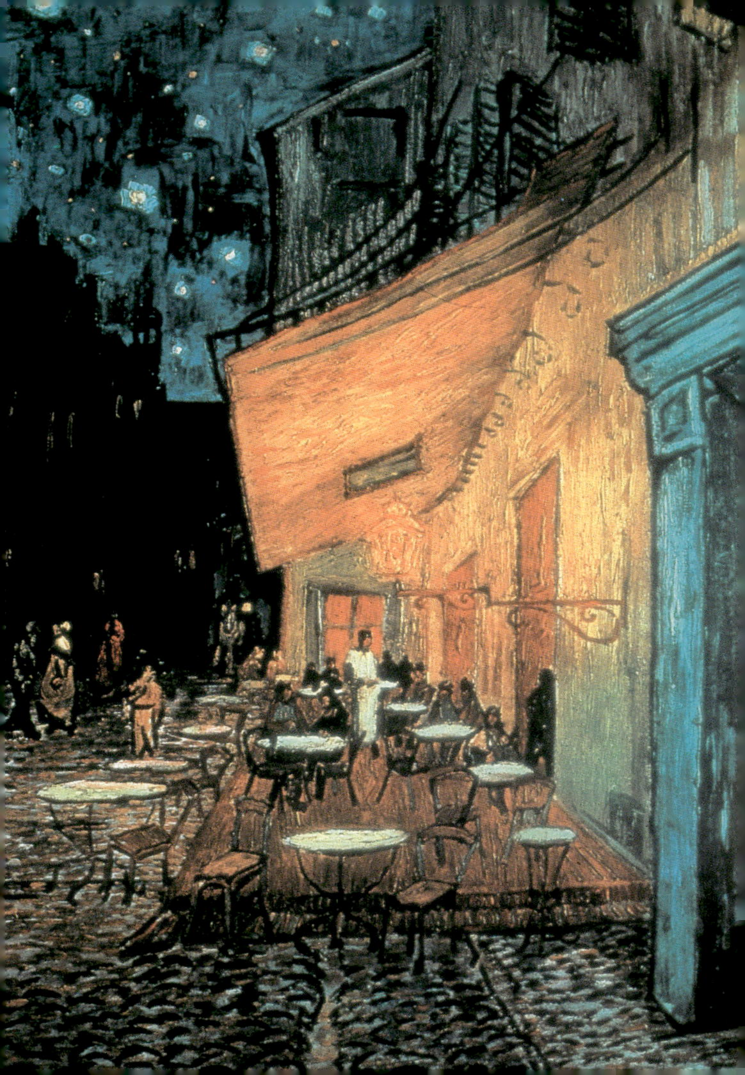

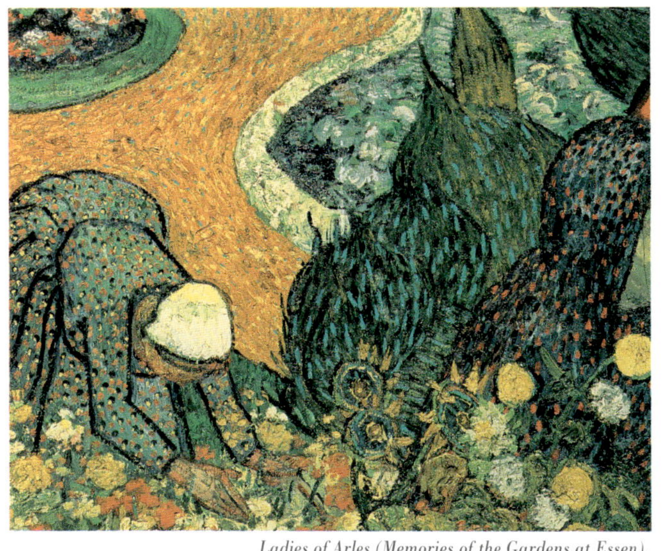

Ladies of Arles (Memories of the Gardens at Essen),
Hermitage Museum, St. Petersburg

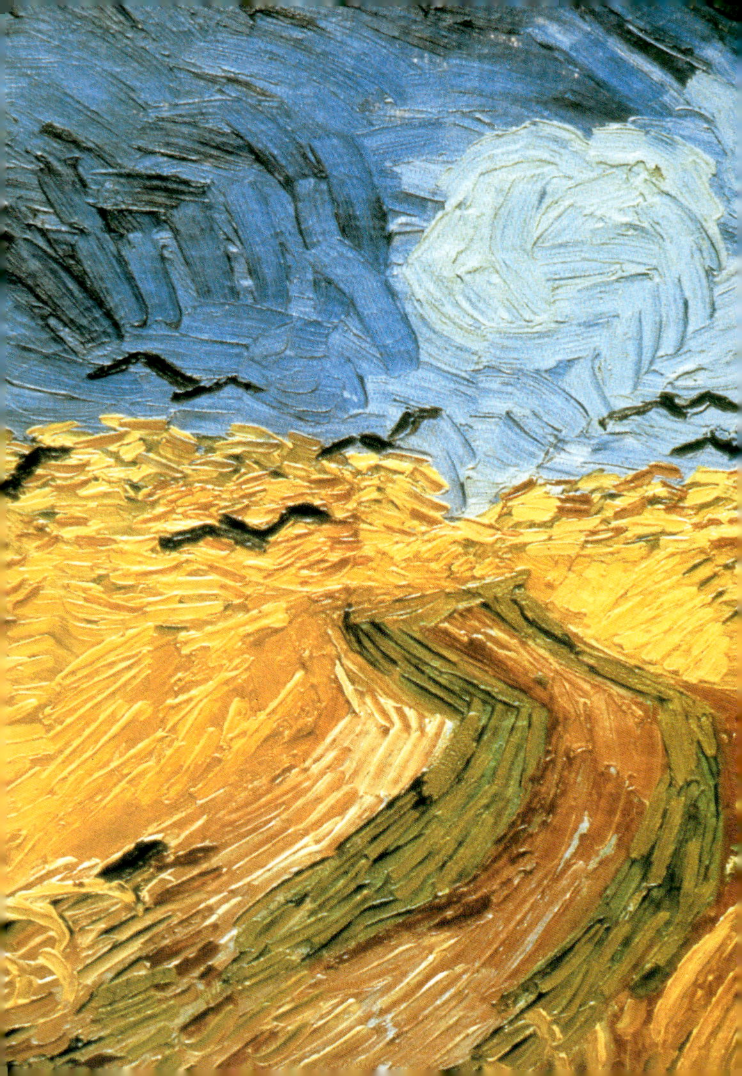

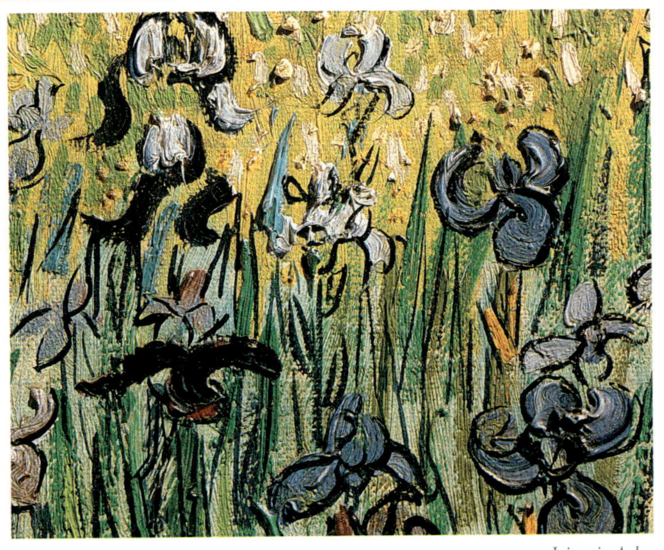

Irises in Arles
Van Gogh Foundation, Amsterdam

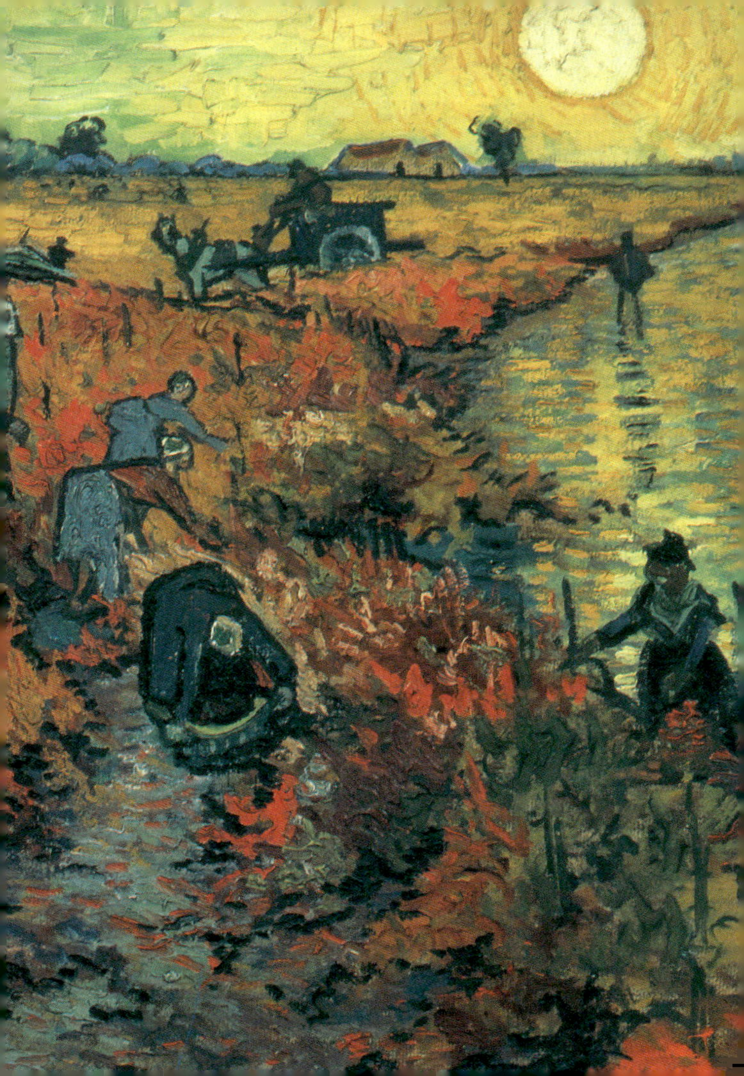

Red Vineyards at Arles,
Pushkin Museum, Moscow

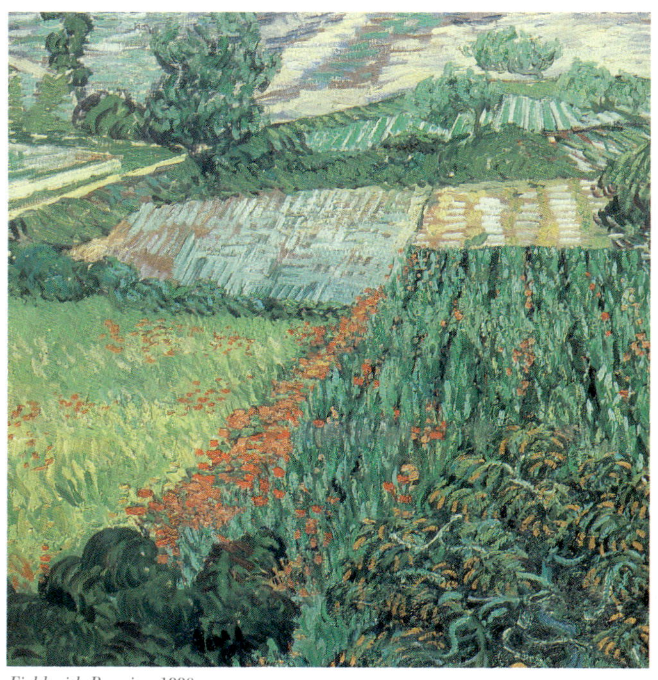

Field with Poppies, 1889
Bremen Art Gallery

A Branch of Chestnut Tree Blossom, 1890
Buhrle Collection, Zurich

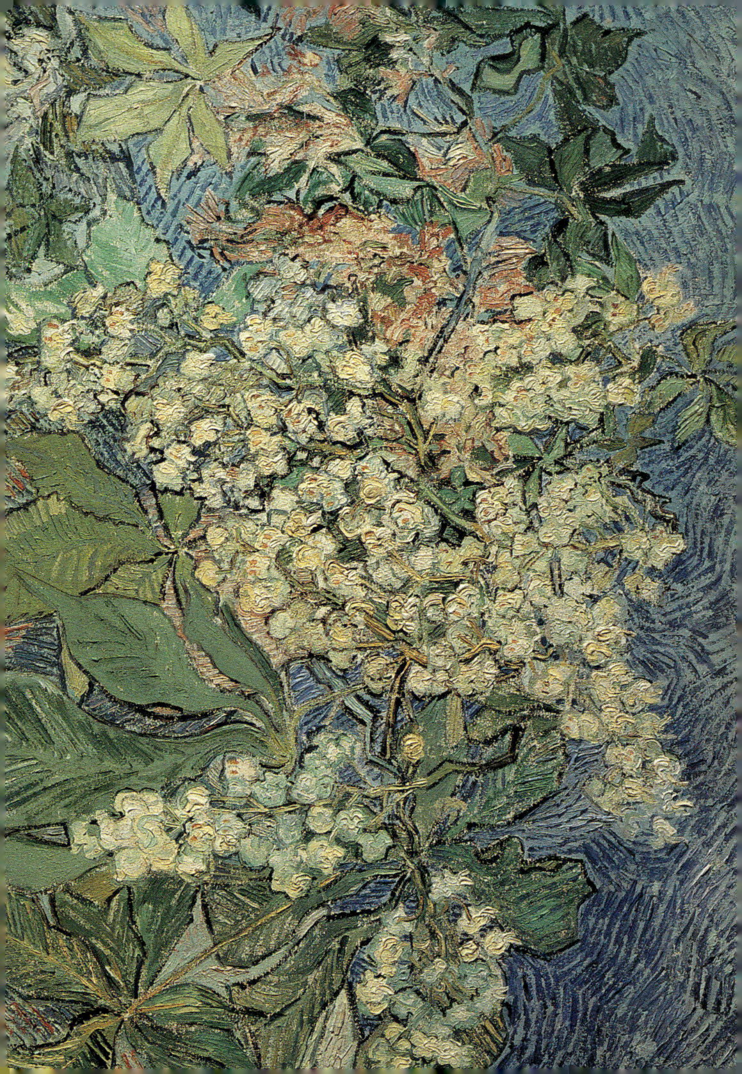

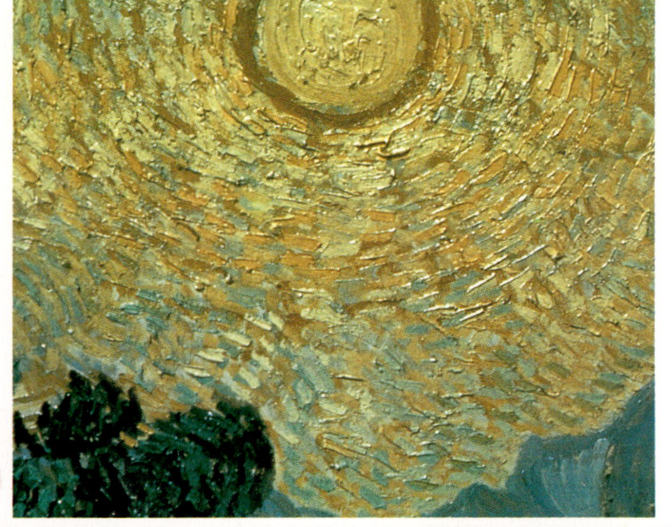

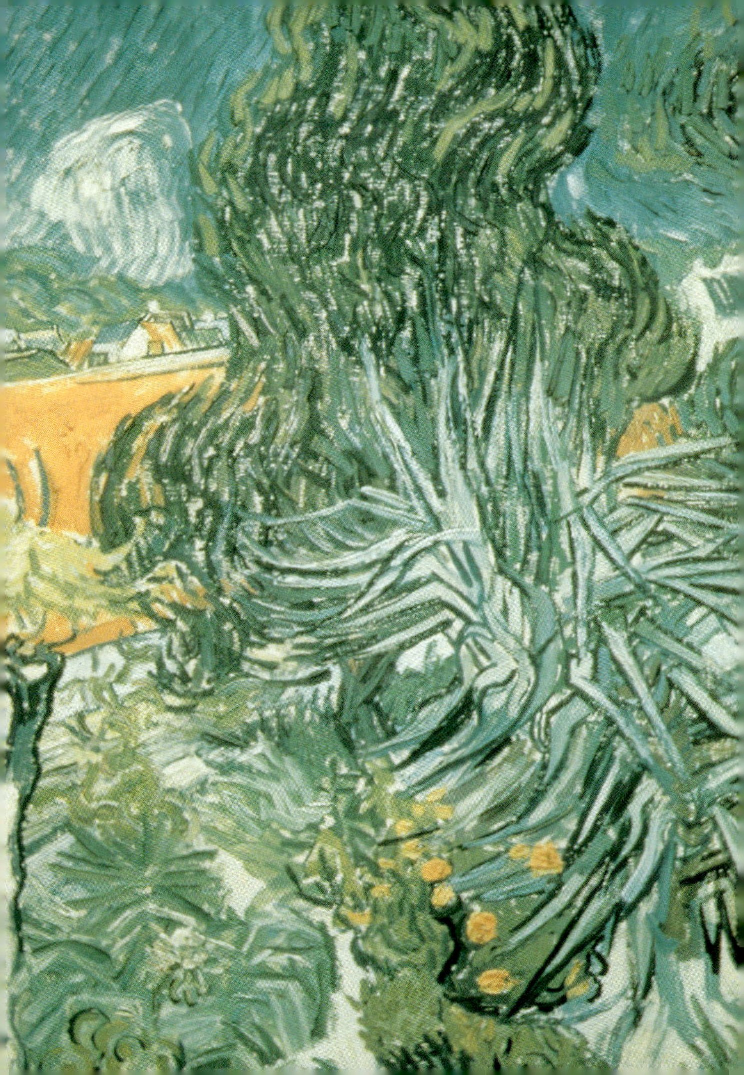

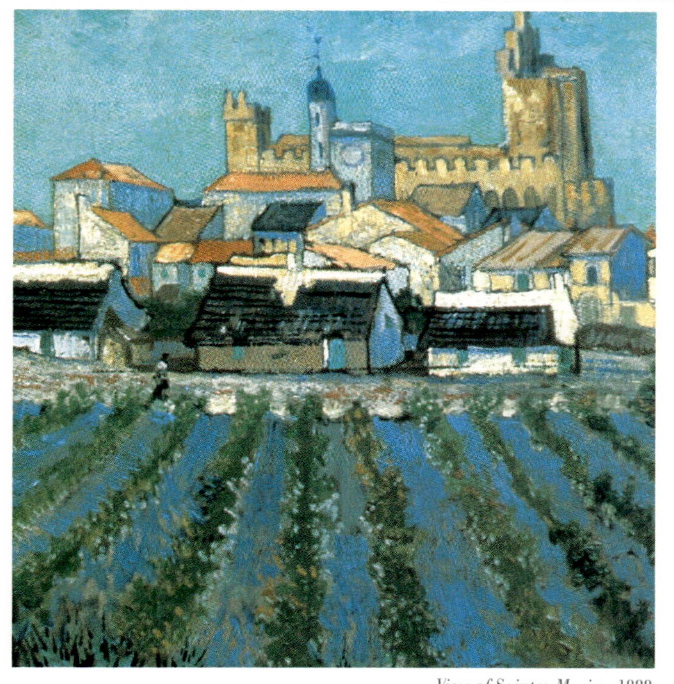

View of Saintes-Maries, 1888
Rijksmuseum Kroeller-Muller, Otterlo

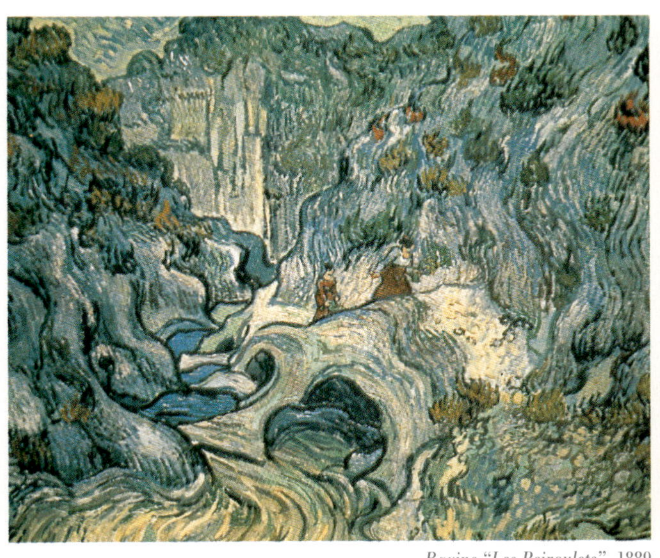

Ravine "Les Peiroulets", 1889
Rijksmuseum Kroeller-Muller, Otterlo

Fritillaries in a Bronze Vase
Private Collection

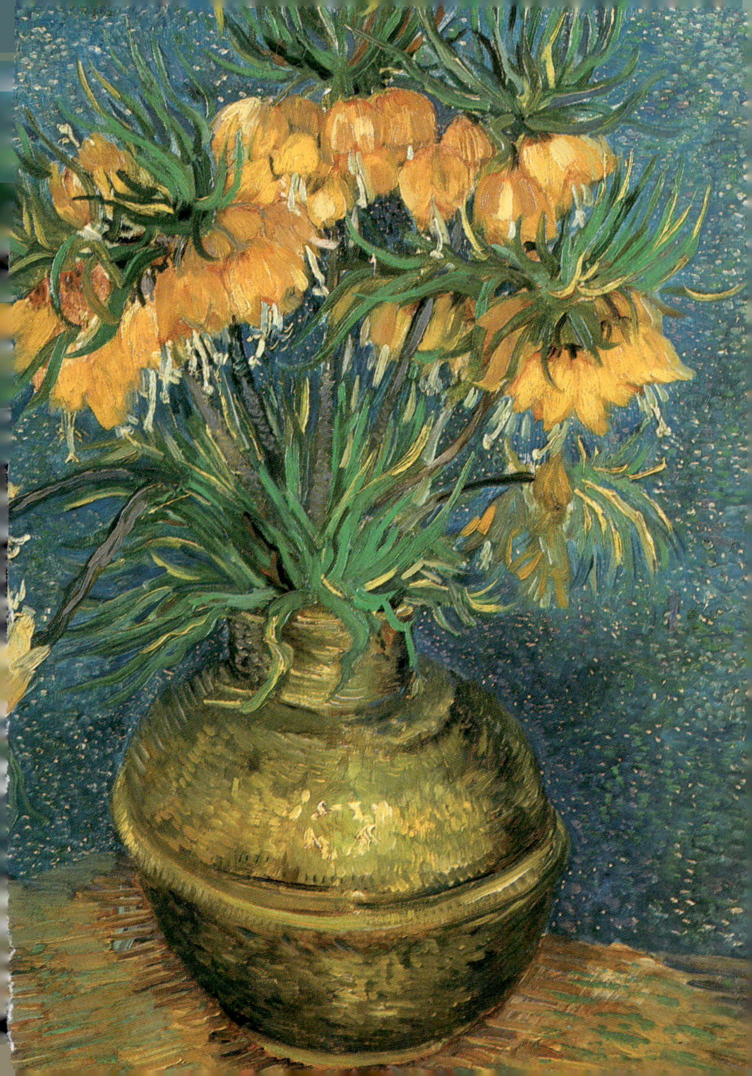

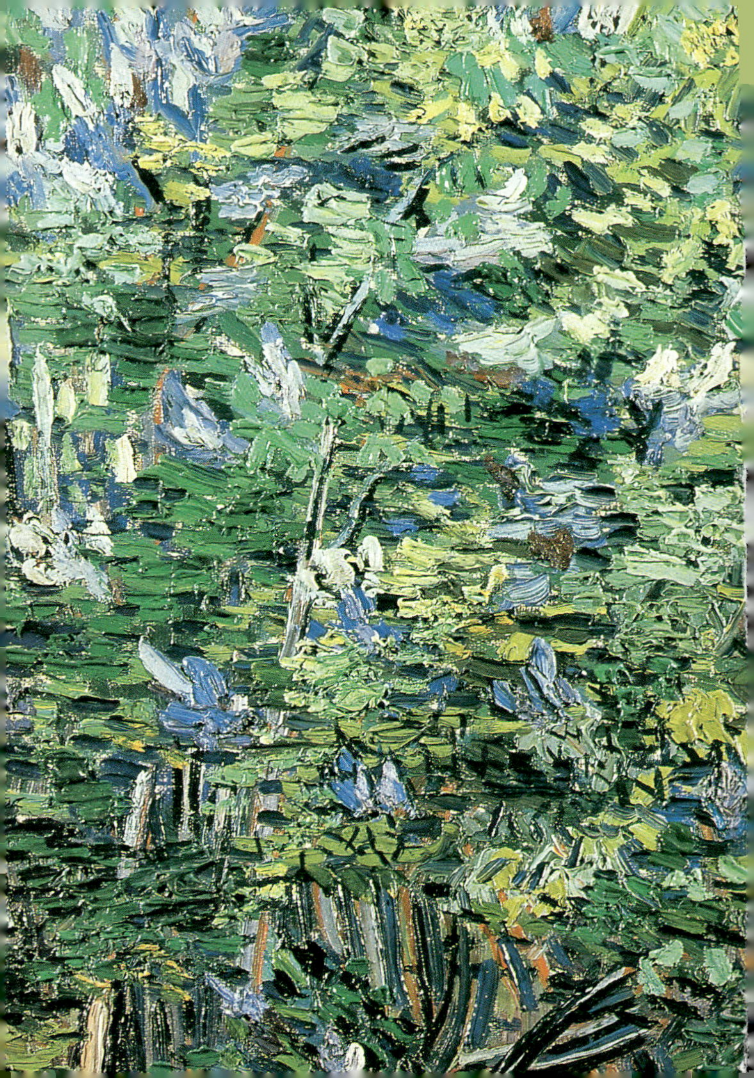